*W*ords from the
MOUNTAIN

by

Robert Cruikshank
Greenville, Alabama

Order this book online at www.trafford.com
or email orders@trafford.com

Most Trafford titles are also available at major online book retailers.

Printed in the United States of America.

ISBN: 978-1-4269-6072-7 (sc)
ISBN: 978-1-4269-6073-4 (e)

Trafford rev. 03/07/2011

 www.trafford.com

North America & international
toll-free: 1 888 232 4444 (USA & Canada)
phone: 250 383 6864 ♦ fax: 812 355 4082

Dedication

The words from the mountain
addressed in these pages
are dedicated
to the glory of Almighty God
and to his only begotten, who is the Christ,
and in loving tribute
to all the saints of every generation
whose lives have been transformed with a new birth of grace
to faithfully embrace and follow in faith and love
the path which leads into our Father's house.
The journey continues
and there remains uncommon deeds to do
in the glorious cause to which believers are called
to wholeheartedly embrace and lovingly share.

Words From the Mountain

Introduction

"UNDERSTANDING THE CALL OF GOD"

Since the beginning of human history, God has called us to be in fellowship and service with him. As our Creator and Father, God has lavished the fullness of his love, his grace, and his glory upon us. In return, he has asked only from us a relationship grounded in the bonds of adoration, thanksgiving, and faithfulness. Such loyal response from us has filled God's heart with honor and joy while blessing our lives with happiness and abundance. It was a neat arrangement. It still is!

The teaching of evolution has in recent years wrecked havoc upon the framework of human society. Its error is that, far from teaching the process of natural selection, or even the theory of how the universe and life came into being; those who embrace it often scoff at the idea that there is a God who has a plan and a purpose for our lives. In short, evolution places *chance* on the throne instead of a just and loving Creator. Chance, however, does not rule our universe. Luck does not control our existence. Fate does not guide our destiny. Our Creator did not bring us into this world to live without a purpose, to exist without a reason, or function without meaning.

In the Genesis story we read about God calling his children in the cool of the evening. It was a time of bliss shared between God and his children, named Adam and Eve. But the relationship between God and his children was soured from an act of their disobedience. They lost their innocence. They had violated their covenant with God and the ensuing guilt with which they clothed themselves in sin and shame forever changed their relationship with their heavenly Father. However, while God, himself, was not changed by Adam and Eve's disobedience, he faced the challenge of restoring them, and their descendants, to their former relationship and state of grace. It was like trying to paste a broken Humpty-Dumpty back together. You probably know the Genesis story well.

However, the important point which we must keep in mind is, first, God has always called out to his children, seeking a covenanted relationship with us. Second, our problem is not that we cannot hear God calling us but, like Adam and Eve, we harbor the notion that we can ignore or delay God's call, continue to do our own thing, and still maintain an open relationship with God on our own terms. Alas, like those first parents, we place ourselves in opposition to God, an estrangement of our own willful choosing, leaving us without a way back home. Third, God remains unchanged and we remain the children of his loving heart. Fourth, as with Adam and Eve, God continues to call out to us in every possible way. All he asks of us is that we abandon our sinful ways in favor of him. God is constantly ready to welcome us home. Fifth, there is not one single reason why each person cannot turn homeward, right now, to the loving heart and the welcoming arms of God, our heavenly Father.

The best way in which I can portray the effect of our rebellion and sin against God is to picture God gowned in a magnificent white robe of holiness. This magnificent white robe represents the whole of God; the entirely of his clean and glorious kingdom. Every sin becomes an ink stain upon the robe, defiling and making it less than sparkling, clean and holy. A holy God cannot abide an ink-stained robe. It is tainted, soiled, ruined. It is less than perfect. Thus, God must cleanse his holy kingdom robe. Every stain must be purged to make the robe perfect and pure again. Now, God can "punish away the stain" by taking his robe to the river and washing it, laying it upon a rock and beating it with a paddle until it becomes pure again. Biblical history reminds us again and again that God has often employed punishment, or a chastising method, of purging away the ink blot or sin which stains his holy kingdom robe. Now, however, instead of punishing away the stain, through the chastisement and death of Jesus Christ, God has perfectly cleansed his royal garment. God's children need no longer be punished. We are forgiven.

Therefore, just as a sinful choice is always ours to make, so is our choice to receive God's forgiveness for our sinful ways. In either case, God will cleanse his royal garment. Thus, the call of God to every person is a call to repent, turn homeward, be cleansed, be forgiven, and become again his children of adoration, thanksgiving, and faithfulness.

But, just as the call of God comes to us, asking us to be his people and to fulfill his will, there are several reasons why we remain reluctant to wholeheartedly trust and obey him. The primary reason we are so reluctant is not because we decline to hear God, or believe him, or trust him. It's because we lack confidence in ourselves. We're afraid God will ask something of us we do not want to do, or something that we cannot do. We're afraid we'll fail, or that others will ridicule us. We're afraid the price will be too great, or that God's call will sidetrack our personal plans.

The Apostle Paul wrote: *"It was he who gave some to be apostles, some to be prophets, some to be evangelists, and some to be pastors and teachers to prepare God's people for works of service, so that the body of Christ may be built up until all reach unity in the faith..."* –Ephesians 4:11-13

God's call comes to each of us, inviting us to become a vital part of his glorious kingdom. The gracious and generous call of God still comes to us through an open door where we are invited to enter, to be reconciled, to be healed and, in return, to offer God our adoration, our thanksgiving, our faithfulness, and our service.

We are called by God and we are called from death to life. We are called to the miracle of salvation and we are called to sanctification. We are called to everlasting life, and we are called to be blessed in this life. We are called to live holy lives, and out of this we are called to do certain tasks. It is in the fulfillment of those varied tasks that the words from the mountain continue to call us and inform us how to live our lives in ways which are pleasing to God and which will bless our lives with treasure beyond measure.

Just keep fixed in mind the words of wisdom my pastor-mentor once shared with me: *"Those whom God calls, God also qualifies."*

CHAPTER 1.

⟊⟊⟊

GOD IDENTIFIES HIMSELF

"I Am who I Am" –Exodus 3:14

The first words from the mountain were spoken by God to Moses, whose appearance to Moses was in the form of a burning bush. Moses observed that the bush was afire, but was not being consumed by the flames. He turned aside for a closer look at that phenomenon and that's when God spoke Moses' name. The account is related in Exodus 3:1-4:17. You probably know the story well. We are told that God had a plan for Moses' life. It was a plan which would deliver the Hebrew people from human bondage. God had set the plan into motion even before Moses had been born. Now, on Mount Horeb, God spoke to Moses and called him to the fulfillment of the plan.

On the heights of Mount Horeb, God identified himself to Moses. When Moses asked, *Suppose I go to the Israelites and say to them, "The God of your fathers has sent me to you," and they ask me, "What is his name?" Then what shall I tell them? God said to Moses, "I am who I am." This is what you are to say to the Israelites: "I AM has sent me to you."* –Exodus 3:13-14.

There we have it! God has identified himself! His name is," *I AM.*"

A full rendition of his name is all inclusive, *"I AM WHO I AM."* The full application of that identity means, *"I have been for you, I am for you, I will be for you."* The sequence in the interpretation of God's name is not a lineal alignment like "past," "present," and "future" stretched out as a time line, abutted end upon end, or year after year, but it is a cylindrical and concentric dimension, somewhat like three coins in a stack wherein "past, present, and future" lie nestled together as a whole within a common sphere. This is what Jesus means when he says, *"I am the Alpha and the Omega' says the Lord God, 'who is, and who was, and is to come'"* (Revelation 1:8). Jesus identifies himself several times in John's Gospel as *"I Am..."* He also says, *"Before Abraham was, I Am"* (John 8:58), and when the Samaritan woman at the well said, "I know that Messiah (called Christ) is coming. When he comes, he will explain everything to us." Then Jesus declared, *"I who speak to you am he"* (John 4:25-26).

Various humanist philosophies and theories about the origin of humankind, and their place on planet earth, have been set forth across the years. Some of those tend to shun God's involvement in creation and laugh at his concern for people. Discounting the creation story, some have hypothesized the human race evolved after the protozoa age from an amoeba in some primeval swamp, became a whale, and finally descended from a monkey who, through some strange and inexplicable freak of nature, matured into a race of human beings. Others point to the discovery of the ancient Cro-Magnon, Neanderthal, or Peking human-like bones and postulate these were ancient ancestors of the human race. Then, there is a conjecture which touts a "big bang" explosion in the sky which originally set the cosmos in motion. While all these speculations are interesting, their hypothesis are wrong because scientific truth is eroded by a conjecture that denies God as the Prime Mover. *If* there was an instantaneous expansion which created the cosmos, scattering planets and universes across distant horizons whereby the solar systems magically began to orbit and function with meticulous precision, there was "someone" whose *presence* created the original atomic structural matter which made such an expansion possible.

The latest theory concerning the creation of mankind attempts to use DNA testing to claim that the human race is descended from a mythical "Adam" of African origin who mysteriously appeared on the world scene around sixty-thousand years ago. The illusion is that around that time period some descendants of that mythical African ancestor crossed 150 miles of ocean and settled in Australia. It adds that a second exodus occurred around 45,000 years ago when another group from Africa settled in the Middle East, with smaller groups going at that time to India, Northern China, and Southern China. Then, around 40,000 years ago, as temperatures warmed and the ice age ended, another group moved to Central Asia. Subsequently, around 35,000 years ago, some smaller groups left Central Asia and migrated to Europe, with yet another smaller group leaving Central Asia around 20,000 years ago to move farther north into Siberia and across the Arctic Circle. The hypothesis is that today's people are two-thousand generations removed from that mythical African "Adam."

What such a theory does is calculate that, given an average of 30 years per generation, there would be two-thousand generations born during that span of sixty-thousand years. It uses that sixty-thousand year time frame as a background to study the migration patterns of the human race, beginning from what it claims is the dawn of human beginning until today. Then, utilizing DNA markers to identify the peoples in those different places as having a common origin, it then relates members of each group to each other group through more ancient identifying DNA markers. If that were the case, there should also be in each spiraled DNA heliograph studied a total of two-thousand generational markers. If, on the other hand, according to the biblical account, the biblical "Adam" and his wife "Eve" did not make their debut until around eight-thousand years ago, with all present peoples of earth being descended from these two persons. Given an average of 40 years per generation, the DNA heliographs should reveal about 150 generational markers. The average of 40 years per generation would seem the more accurate figure considering that the males of the first one-hundred generations were usually much older when their succeeding generation was birthed, with the last fifty-generations of males being much younger when their families were begun. While the study of DNA is interesting, the time line seems to be one of conjecture with the DNA testing results skewed to fit the time frame hypothesis.

Thus, some social scientists, archeologists, and paleontologists have made, and continue to make, these types of errors and conjectures their imbalanced diet of faulty reasoning. There still exists a fierce determination by some to defy and disprove the biblical account. Either they create their own doubt and then agree with it, or they begin with the wrong hypotheses. In much the same way doubters, deniers, and theorists often look at the human social dilemma and advocate "fixing" evil and wrongdoing through the advent of reasoning, government, and law.

While these have their place in an ordered society, this book does not look to the established disciplines of science or the humanities as a means of fixing "what's wrong," but looks to Yahwah, the Lord of all creation, the great *"I AM"* who spoke to Moses from a burning bush, and then endeavors to help us see "what's right." It calls us again to have faith in these words from the mountain, which God spoke to Moses, as the hope and cure for our spiritual truancy. Faith in God is not the crowning of some concocted philosophy, but once we have faith we can philosophize about it. In other words, once we have faith in God and address our human dilemma through his teachings, we are empowered by God to address sin and evil and then choose the more noble responses which both honor God and benefit human society. The words spoken by God to Moses is the impetus by which human life can be successfully ordered for the benefit of all peoples. Until that day fully emerges, however, society must content itself to rely upon the substitutes of reasoning, government, and law as a means of coercing society to order itself.

Admittedly, we do not know from whence God came or how he came to be. Early catechisms proclaim that God exists but they do not attempt to probe his specific time or place of appearing. As to God's origin, the ancient scriptures merely proclaim that God exists. And those scriptures offer a surrogate name called *heaven"* as God's place of residence. What we do know, however, is that where we now exist – our earth, its solar system, the cosmos – there once was nothing; a vacuum. The Book of Genesis describes it as a *"void,"* and says that *"God created..."* In other words, where once there was nothing, God made something! One probing question would be to ask, *"How did God do that?"* A more elusive and more pertinent inquiry might be, *"Why did God do that?"*

The foundation for an awareness of, and having faith in, the great "I Am," the God of the mountain who spoke to Moses, is based in the conviction that God was, and continues to be, the Prime Mover, the Creator of our lives, and where we exist (earth, its solar system, the cosmos), there once was nothing, which the Book of Genesis calls a void, literally a vacuum. Genesis tells us that, *"God created."* In other words, God made something where once there was nothing.

Creation and evolution are not enemies on opposite ends of the spectrum; they are compatible. Yet, even in their continuity, they are two different things. Creation is about origin while evolution is about the subsequent process of that which was originated at the dawn of beginning. This is what makes creation a living, breathing, ongoing process. Therefore, it is not difficult to understand that the God of first creation also established a process for his creation to evolve and grow. And, it is reasonable to conclude that the Cro-Magnon, Neanderthal, or Peking beings are as extinct as the dinosaurs, while the race of human beings now occupying earth came into existence only a few thousand years ago. We are a new creation residing in a new reign on an ancient planet. We are part of the Creator's continuing, growing, process.

In consequence, we should completely believe this God of the mountain by taking his creation into account. And, when we consider creation, including everything which has been created, we ultimately end up dealing with atoms and atomic structures whose tiny, unseen, but detectable bits of *matter* are the diet of scientists. But, even the nonscientific mind can grasp their royal place within creation. Almost everybody understands that all things seeable and touchable consists of some form of matter or some structural combination of matter, whether that matter is located in earthly deposits or in the far reaches of space and the cosmos. What is important to understand is that everything physical which exists consists of matter.

Elementary science has long known, however, that an atom is not an atom by itself. Each atom is a nucleus of smaller matter, which can be measured. Every atom also contains an immeasurable and non-weighable amount of Energy, in the sense we measure and weigh matter. Science has also used many names to identify this energy. I choose to believe that this non-material energy is *a Presence,* and more specifically, God's Presence in his Holy Spirit. I draw the conclusion that it was with this "Presence" by which God created the heavens and the earth and all things on the earth. In the beginning, God created all matter out of nothing. I believe God has the power to do that. God made it, he still holds the deed, and it belongs to him.

Now, the first law of thermodynamics says that no mass or energy is ever destroyed; it merely changes form. When a piece of wood is burned, it is not gone. Some of it is transformed into heat; some deteriorates into ashes. But is it not destroyed, it just changes. When a lake dries up, the water is gone. It is transformed into steam, evaporated into the atmosphere only to fall to earth again somewhere as rain. If we can grasp this transformation process of matter taking place around us in the physical world, it is not difficult to grasp its spiritual significance.

Science should also understand that, while this Presence holds matter together, if the Presence were to be removed, instead of matter simply collapsing and falling apart, matter itself would cease to exist. Neither would it leave an identifiable empty space where it once existed. Instead, there would be nothing, a complete void. In other words, if this Presence were to be completely withdrawn from our planet, Earth would not fly into a zillion pieces of star dust floating in space, the earth would cease to exist as if it had never been and the space which earth now occupies would be a void, a place where creation ceases to exist. God's withdrawal of his creative *"Presence"* or Holy Spirit would be the exact opposite of creation. It is comforting to know that God is a creator and not a destroyer, but If we can fathom the manner in which creation could cease to exist, it is not that difficult to believe those Biblical words, *"In the beginning God created the heavens and the earth. Now the earth was formless and empty, darkness was over the surface of the deep and the Spirit of God was hovering over the waters."* Then, God said *"Let there be..."* , and created *'matter,'* with its aura of God's *Presence* , appeared where once there was nothing. *(Genesis1:1-3 NIV).* It is time for us to believe the One who spoke to Moses. We would do well to hear anew, and urgently incorporate into our lives, his words from the mountain,

"I Am Who I Am."

Chapter 2.

<hr>

CHOOSE THE RIGHT GOD

"I am the Lord your God, who brought you out of Egypt, out of the land of slavery. You shall have no other gods before me..."
—Exodus 20:2-3

These are also words from the mountain. They are words spoken to Moses and they were chiseled in stone. We know that when something is chiseled in stone, it cannot be changed. But we have a long history of attempting to alter or soften the meaning of God's words, if not wholly endeavoring to change them. But regardless of how much some people in every generation have tried to change them, or excuse them, or dilute and water them down, they cannot because they were first etched in stone. Afterwards, Moses bade the Hebrew people memorize these words, to etch them in their hearts, so they could teach them to later generations. Someone in every generation has always remembered the words from the mountain and honored them as God's superior way to peace, joy, and happiness.

In his letter to the Romans the Apostle Paul touches on our otherwise vain efforts when he says:

"The wrath of God is being revealed from heaven against all the godlessness and wickedness of men who suppress the truth by their wickedness, since what may be known about God is plain to them, because God has made it plain to them. For since the creation of the world God's invisible qualities–his eternal power and divine nature– have been clearly seen, being understood from what has been made, so that men are without excuse. For although they knew God, they neither glorified him as God nor gave thanks to him, but their thinking became futile and their foolish hearts were darkened. Although they claimed to be wise, they became fools and exchanged the glory of the immortal God for images made to look like mortal man and birds and animals and reptiles." (Romans 1:8-23)

The words from the mountain were chiseled in stone and, therefore, were unchangeable. We know the story well. How Moses had been born of Hebrew parents but raised from his childhood by Pharaoh's daughter. Upon discovering his Hebrew birthright, Moses incurred trouble for himself over Egyptian injustice for the Hebrew people. Moses killed an Egyptian taskmaster, after which he fled to the land of Median and, in the land of Median, married the daughter of Jethro.

One day, while tending Jethro's sheep, Moses saw a burning bush. Upon seeing that the bush was not being consumed by the flames, Moses approached it. It was then that God spoke to Moses out of the burning bush. From that encounter with God, Moses was sent back to Egypt to free the Hebrew's from their slavery. We know the story of the Hebrew's release and their crossing the Red Sea. We know about their struggles and the many miracles given to them by God during their journey. They were fed manna during their wilderness journey, and given water from a rock. A cloud of dust guided them by day, and a pillar of fire by night. When they arrived at Mount Sinai, God spoke to Moses again, and his words were chiseled in stone.

"I am the Lord your God, who brought you out of Egypt, out of the land of slavery. You shall have no other gods before me..."
- Deuteronomy 5:6-7

For those Hebrews, and for us, there has been a long history with a wide-range of falsely chosen gods. A parable about making wrong choices is told by Jotham, the youngest son of Jerub-Baal. The parable, found in Judges 9:8-15, relates how, one day, the trees went out to choose a king for themselves. They first approached the olive tree to become their king, then the fig tree, then the vine, but these all had more important work to do producing oil, fruit, and wine. Neither of these three had time to go about waving their branches over the other trees. Finally, all the trees said to the bramble bush, "Come and be our king." The bramble bush readily agreed to become their king, providing the other trees would take refuge in his shade, but if they failed to make him their king, "..then let fire come out of the bramble bush and consume the cedars of Lebanon." The wider scope of this parable can be applied to our selection of the gods we choose as well as the earthly leaders to whom we pledge our allegiance.

Take a few moments to respond to the following:
–Can you name some of the ancient gods of the world?
–Can you identify some of the gods revered by today's society?
–What do some people think these gods could do for them?
–What can any single god from this array of contrived gods do?
–Is the name of Yahwah, the God who spoke to Moses, among those listed?

Well, henceforth, for the Hebrew people, the name of God was to be known as YHWH. That name, by which they were to know God, did not have vowels. Thus, they were unable to pronounce God's name because the Hebrew people believed God to be so holy that it was improper for them to speak his name. Thereafter, where YHWH appears in the ancient scriptures it is rendered as Lord, with a capitol **L**. Later on, God was always referred to as Jahwah or Yahwah, from which the name, *"Jehovah,"* is derived.

Now, among all the known gods of ancient times, and all the modern gods many people have adopted and kneel before today, who is the one whom you choose to worship and serve? Why?

The Great Commandment (Deut. 6:4-19) is called the *"Shema,"* which comes from the Hebrew language and is translated, *"Hear."* It begins:

"Hear, O Israel, the Lord our God, the Lord is one. Love the Lord your God with all your heart and with all your might and with all your strength" (Deut. 6:4-5). *." Fear the Lord your God and serve him only..."* (Deut. 6:13).

These translated words, *The Lord our God, the Lord is one,"* as written in Hebrew, literally reads, *"Yahweh,* our *God, Yahweh, One."*

The words, *"Love the Lord your God..."* attempts to avoid a legalism of obedience based on necessity and duty, implying that *"we should love the Lord because he first loved us."* The Scriptures, however, teach us that *love without obedience is not true love.* This obedience includes our reverence, devotion, honesty, and fidelity in all our relationships and our undertakings.

This is particularly noted when, during his wilderness temptation, Jesus said: *"...away from me Satan! For it is written: 'worship the Lord your God, and serve him only'"* –Matthew 4:10.

Here, it is important for us to understand that "God" is an English word, translated and derived from a root word meaning "to call," and indicates simply the object of our worship; the one whom we call upon or invoke.

It is important to note that *the Nature of God* has revealed himself in three ways:

First, as infinite Presence, or Lord of the natural order of all things. This is creating love. Second, as Savior of the lost, or the Lord who bestows grace. This is redeeming love. Third, as Triune Being, or God the Father, Son, and Holy Spirit. This is witnessing love.

It was this God, Yahwah, who spoke to Moses from the burning bush and later, on Sinai, provided to Moses and the Hebrew people the Ten Commandants, the first of which is:

"I am the Lord your God, who brought you out of Egypt, out of the land of slavery. You shall have no other gods before me..." –Deut. 5:6-7

Choose the God of creation, who made heaven and earth and all things upon the earth. Choose the God and Father of our Lord Jesus Christ, who loves us so much that he gave his only begotten Son, that whoever believes in him shall not perish but have eternal life. Both, choose Him, then get to know him. Discover how the Creator of the universe loves, listens, and heals. See him as he guards, guides, and gives. Listen to him as he instills, instructs, and increases. Choose to worship and follow, and to trust and obey, the one true God who is ever ancient, yet always new.

In other words, what God was saying from the mountain to Moses, and to us, is this:

"Choose the Right God!"

CHAPTER 3.

REMAIN FOCUSED

"You shall not make for yourself any substitutes..."
Exodus 20:4

These words, spoken from the mountain by God to Moses, Exodus 20:1-17, and Deuteronomy 5:6-21, are included among those "chiseled in stone" words.

Later, when the Hebrew people encamped in a valley outside the city of Beth-Peor, a temple of the Moabites, from the place where they were then standing they could gaze upon the temple of an idol god. Moses had called a temporary halt to the Hebrew's exhausting march and had gathered around himself the whole assembly of the people, who he calls "All Israel." The tribal elders and as many of the people who were able came within hearing range of Moses. The greatest among them were not above God's command, nor were the least of them below God's comfort.

Although the words from God had been spoken previously, and chiseled in stone, Moses is here requiring that the words of the covenant be rehearsed again by the people of God. Moses knew that in order for all the people to remember, and not forget, precept had to be forged upon precept, line upon line, rehearsed again and again, sufficient enough to keep the words of God fixed within their hearts and minds. It was not their fathers, but they, who had made a covenant with the Lord. It was they and their descendants who must keep the covenant they had made.

"You shall not make for yourself any substitutes..."

In other words, having chosen the right God, this admonishment is to stay focused in our choice. It is vital that we keep our hearts and our lives fixed upon our one true God; our creator and friend. There will be serious consequences should we lose our focus on Yahwah, the God of the Mountain.

This second commandment concerns the way in which God is to be worshiped. No idols are permitted! The prohibition includes the making of images, even of the Lord, himself. We are called upon to remember the Lord our God by faith, and to worship him by faith. Faith and nothing else, is intended to be the basic core of our relationship with, and our service to, God. He is to be held in our hearts and minds, not in our seeing eyes. Our seeing eyes, however, are to behold the mighty works which the Lord our God does among us.

Matthew Henry's Commentary, vol. 1, p.359, says: "Though worship was designed to terminate in God, it would not please him if it came to him through an image. The best and most ancient lawgivers among the heathens forbade the setting up of images in their temples. This practice was forbidden in Rome by Nuda, a pagan prince, yet commanded in Rome by the pope, a Christian bishop, but, is this, anti-Christian? The use of images in the church of Rome, at this day is so plainly contrary to the letter of this command, and so impossible to be reconciled to it, that in all their catechisms and books of devotion which they put into the hands of the people, they leave out this commandment, joining the reason of it to the first, and so the third commandment they call the second, the third the fourth, etc..."

In light of this statement, there are several important questions which our society must address and resolve:

–What were some of the graven images worshiped among ancient peoples?

–What might be considered to be graven images which are employed today?

–Is there a difference between a graven image and a religious symbol?

Is the Crucifix itself a graven image or a religious symbol?

Is the Cross?

Baptism? The Eucharist?

–When is the line crossed between graven images and religious symbols?

–What may be some problems regarding pluralism and political correctness?

–Can a Christian be politically correct, yet be obedient to the 1st Commandment?

–Should there be prayer in public school? If so, when? Where?

By whom?

From the outset, there were two obstacles which the Hebrew people had to overcome. The first obstacle was their fear of God. The Hebrews had been filled with extreme terror and consternation by the manner in which these chiseled in stone words were received from God. When Moses received the Ten Commandments on Mt. Sinai, that rendition had been accompanied by billowing smoke, belching flames, thunder, and lightening.

Now, they are being compelled by Moses to repeat and memorize these words whereby they could recall to their minds that awesome appearing of the Lord. Their first impulse was to put the Lord's visitation out of their minds. Their awe of God's appearing was so great they considered it as no immediate comfort to them.

Not recalling the Lord, however, would eventually result in their forgetting God, thus they would be unable to pass along to their children and grandchildren the Covenant which they had made with the Lord. This brings into focus for us the instructions by Jesus to his disciples, "..do this in Remembrance of me" -Luke 22:19. The Hebrew root of the word "Remember" is zaw-kar, meaning "to mark" or to "think on." The Greek word, "anamnesis," comes from a Greek root which literally means "to recall or bring forth as if actually present." Ironically, the word "amnesia," meaning to forget, comes from the same Greek root word.

By Moses' having them repeat the Lord's Commandments until memorized, the Hebrew people would soon realize that God would not destroy or harm them. And, they would remember and teach the succeeding generations knowledge and obedience to the Lord through these words. The Hebrew children would soon go forward to inherit the Promised Land and, while Moses would not accompany them to that place, he made certain that the people and their succeeding generations would remember, whereby they might keep intact, these words from the mountain.

The second obstacle which the Hebrew people faced was their exposure to foreign gods. The armies which opposed the Hebrews were about to be defeated and the Hebrews were about to take the reigns of governing the land. However, there were survivors of those peoples dwelling in those lands who worshiped idol gods instead of Yahwah. The land in which they were to live would have the culture of two societies. There would be danger involved in the social interchange between the two different cultures.

The greater danger, however, was spiritual. The absorption into their lives, and consequently into Hebrew worship, of those lingering cultural traces of idol worship practices presented a problem. A mixing of the two would result in a homogenized religion created by the people, which would degrade Yahwah, be an affront to him, and remove the Hebrew people from his promised protection and grace.

The danger with which the Hebrews was confronted also poses problems for today's society. The following inquires should be fully considered:

   –Can two cultures live intermingled in residency and still
     remain totally apart from each other?
   –If so, How would we manage separate trade, currency, or
     city services?
   –How would we fund education, medical services, or leisure
     activities?
   –Can we expect from God such a thing called, "total
     independence," or
     Is independence the responsibility of persons or nations
     to decide and manage their own internal affairs?
   –What do we do with religion? What about faith? Is faith
     private or public?
   –What did God expect from Moses and the Hebrew people?
     What does God expect of us?

For one thing, God expected devout loyalty and obedience from Moses and the Hebrew people. He expects no less from us.

—a devout loyalty to him means, "you shall have no other gods before me..." In other words, *choose the right God.*
—a devout obedience to him means, "you shall not make for yourself any substitutes..." *stay focused.*

Helen H. Lemmel's hymn places new flesh upon the words of God spoken from the mountain to Moses, words which Moses impressed upon the Hebrew people and words which we would also do well to hear and heed:

"Turn your eyes upon Jesus, look full in his wonderful face, and the things of life will grow strangely dim, in the light of his glory and grace."

John Wesley once advised his Methodist followers to, "Work out your own salvation." In whatever way we do that, by whatever means it takes, it is imperative that we make the right choices. And, in the choices which we are called upon to make every day, Yahwah expects us to...

"Remain Focused On Him in All Our Undertakings."

CHAPTER 4.

KEEP IT CLEAN

"You shall not misuse the name of the Lord your God..."
—Exodus 20:7

The King James Version says: "Thou shalt not <u>take</u> the name of the Lord thy God in vain..." The Revised Standard Version says: "You shall not make <u>wrongful use</u> of the name of the Lord your God..." The New International Version says: "You shall not <u>misuse</u> the name of the Lord your God..." The Modern Living Version says: "You shall not <u>use</u> the name of the Lord your God profanely..." The Living Bible Version says: "You must never <u>use</u> my name to make a vow you don't intend to keep..."

The words, <u>take</u> and <u>not use</u>, are translated from the ancient Hebrew word, *"naw-saw,"* which means "to lift," and has many applications. For example in Psalm 4:6 we find the following translated differences:

"Lord, lift thou up the light of thy countenance upon us..." (KJV)

"Let the light of your face shine on us, O Lord..." (RSV)

"Let the light of your face shine upon us, O Lord..." (NIV)

Also, the word, *"naw-saw,"* is translated variously throughout the Old Testament as: *accept* (Job 13:8,10), *advance* (Es. 5:11), *able to* (Gen. 13:6), *bear* (Gen. 4:13), *bring* (forth) (Gen. 45:19), *carry* (away) (Is. 30:6), *contain* (Ezr. 45:11), *ease* (Job 7:13), *exact* Neh. 5:7), *exalt* (Dan. 11:14 , *extol* (Isa. 52:13), *fetch* (Job 36:3), *forgive* (Isa. 2:9), *furnish* (1 Ki. 9:11), *further* (Ezr. 8:36), *give* (2 Sam. 19:42), + *help, high, hold up, lade, lay, lift* (self) *up, lofty, marry, magnify, needs, obtain, pardon, raise* (up), *receive, regard, respect, set* (up), *spare, stir up, swear, take* (away) (up), *wear, yield, etc...*

First, however, the meaning of this third word spoken by God to Moses concerns right use of the Lord's name. Profanity is forbidden. The use of God's name in an improper context is not acceptable. For example,

"God, what a sight," falls short of divine meaning.

"O God, what a sight," may, on the other hand, actually be uttered as a prayer in which the speaker is offering thanksgiving for a beautiful sunrise , or is beginning a plea regarding a disaster., etc. The point is, we should be very careful in choosing our words so their intent is perfectly clear.

An often debated point is when a witness in a courtroom proceeding is asked to "swear" or "affirm" to their truthful testimony by holding up their right hand and declaring: "I swear to tell the truth, the whole truth, and nothing but the truth, so help me God!" At first glance, we ask: "Does this uphold or violate the 3rd Commandment? Is God uplifted by truthful testimony, or is the attester guilty of swearing by God?

Second, the deeper meaning in Exodus 20:7 is concerned that we have within ourselves "a right attitude" toward God. Clearly, the attitude of the Hebrews toward Yahwah was required to be more than uttered words. The language of their attitudes, their personalities, and their labors, was to reflect completely their "reverence" of Yahwah, their Creator and Lord.

Yahwah was more than some innate object toward whom they were to address their affection. He was their Creator and the Hebrews were called upon, and pledged, to recognize God's omnipotence. Thus, Moses outlined for them, in these words from the mountain, articles designed for them to remember which would guide them in fulfilling their relationship with God and with one another.

Third, the meaning intended in Exodus 20:7 requires that God be taken seriously. Moses and the Hebrews were not given the option of picking and choosing between likes and dislikes. God had spoken, his words were chiseled in stone, and the only choice given the Hebrews was, "Yes!" or "No!" They could yield obedience to Yahwah, or reject him. Choosing to believe, worship and serve Yahwah meant that he would protect and prosper them. To reject Yahwah would be to deny and renounce all that they had witnessed during their journey from Egypt.

God's message from the mountain was simple: "I am the Lord thy God - Keep it Clean!" Keep your worship clean. Keep your language clean. Keep your relationships clean. My creation is holy and pure! I made it that way! Now take care of it! Be sincere in everything you say! Be sincere in everything you do!

Keep it clean! Do not use my name in any manner which does not honor me. Such usage profanes me. Do not use my name to pretend something that you don't mean. That also profanes me. Do not use my name, or anything connected with me and my creation, to make a mess and then call it something else, because that profanes me greatly.

–How do you think God feels when profanity is used in language? Why?

–How do you think God feels when we make a promise but fail to keep it?

–Can you think of promises we make, or make in God's name, but fail to keep?

–How do you suppose God feels about that? What are the consequences?

–Is there a connection between speaking and using God's name in our speech, speaking or using God's name in our actions, and the way we relate to people, animals, plants, and natural resources, as well as things in our everyday lives?

–Think of some ways in which the environment may, as part of our language and behavior, be utilized for the glory of God?

–Can the environment be exploited for personal gain in violation of the third Commandment?

–What may be the consequences of environmental utilization and exploitation?

–How do you think God feels about the utilization of his creation?

–How Can we keep it clean? Is that really necessary or important!

Whatever other questions we might frame, the correct response will always be the same; respectfully honor the name of the Lord your God and...

"Keep it Clean!"

CHAPTER 5.

❦

STAY IN TOUCH

"Remember the Sabbath day by keeping it holy..."
—Exodus 20:8

The first mention of the Sabbath is found in Exodus 16:23, when the Hebrew people were in the wilderness, living on manna and quail which the Lord provided each morning.

"Each morning everyone gathered as much as he needed, and when the sun grew hot, it melted away. On the sixth day, they gathered twice as much – two omers for each person – and the leaders of the community came and reported this to Moses. He said to them, this is what the Lord commanded: 'Tomorrow is to be a day of rest, a Holy Sabbath to the Lord. So bake what you want to bake and boil what you want to boil. Save whatever is left and keep it until morning.' So they saved it until morning, as Moses commanded, and it did not stink or get maggots in it. 'Eat it today,' Moses said,' because today is a Sabbath to the Lord." –Exodus 16:23

The Hebrew word for *Sabbath* is "Shabbath" (shab-bawth), meaning: *"intermission."*

The word *"Shabbath"* is derived from the Hebrew word <u>"sha-bath"</u> (pronounced shaw-bath), meaning to repose, or to desist from exertion. That word first appearing in Genesis 2:2-3, is translated as *"rested."*

"..by the seventh day God had finished the work he had been doing; so on the seventh day he <u>'rested'</u> from all his work. And God blessed the seventh day and made it holy, because on it he <u>'rested'</u> from all the work of creating that he had done." –Genesis 2:2-3

No one can be certain which day the first *Sabbath* or *day of rest* precisely was, but by the time these scriptures were written a calendar had been developed as a means for keeping track of time. The year was arranged into four seasons which, in turn, were arranged into weeks and days. Within early calendar systems, based on position of the sun and moon, were established seasonal holiday celebrations or events, which also helped each culture define their calendar. Early calendars were not precise, however, and have since undergone several modifications.

We cannot help but wonder, did the amazing and exacting work of God in creating a calendar week of seven days work very nicely into the early Hebrew religious scheme or did the Hebrews have precise information about which days were the first or the seventh day of creation? Whatever the answer might be, it seems that early cultures were in agreement with the calendar system, even to the point of recognizing and naming each of those seven different days of the week. A particular day's name might be differently named, but its number was always the same.

The Hebrew *Sabbath* is our Saturday, and extends from Friday evening until Saturday evening. The reason for the haste by Joseph of Arimathea to bury the body of Jesus was because the *Sabbath* was upon them and it would not be possible to bury him after sundown on that crucifixion Friday. Jesus' *resurrection* occurred on <u>the first day</u> of the week, and from earliest times *the followers of Jesus gathered on Sunday (the first day) to celebrate his resurrection.* The followers of Christ are *A Resurrection People.*

The Hebrew word for *"keep,"* as in keep the sabbath, is *"Shawmar."* It literally means to *hedge,* or to *hedge in.* It is here translated as *"observe,"* or *"keep".*

When God proclaimed his words from the mountain to Moses, he delivered them in a logical sequence in terms of progressive importance, beginning with the most vital step, with each succeeding commandment gaining its strength from those preceding commandments. This forth commandment serves like a hinge separating the first three commandments and the succeeding six commandments. Take a moment to trace again the first three of these progressive steps:

–*The First Commandment is to Choose the Right God.*
–*The Second Commandment is to Remain Focused.*
–*The Third Commandment is to Keep it Clean.*

While these first three commandments deal with a proper relationship between ourselves and God, the final six commandments deal with a proper relationship between ourselves and others. Hence, the fourth commandment is a requirement for us to *Stay in Touch with God.* Every person should be in constant touch with God, in a moment-by-moment relationship, but this special set-aside time also includes the community-at-large. It is a special time to be set aside by the community in acknowledgment of the Lord; a time to worship, praise, pray, petition, and learn. This set-aside time also permits God to be in touch with the community, providing opportunity for the Lord's Spirit to influence, to speak, touch, assure, guide, renew, strengthen, and to instruct the assembled people. It is a time to be clothed from above with God's love; that the assembled people may be more loving to others.

The effect of remaining in touch with God is that, while God gets the glory, we receive the benefits. Should we fail to give God glory, however, our benefits are reduced accordingly. When God is honored, we are the ones who are lifted up. The downside is that if we choose to live like gutter rats, we neglect God. The choice is ours to make but if we want to honor God, to honor ourselves, and to honor others, we do so when we stay in touch with God and keep the Sabbath.

It doesn't take a genius to grasp the effect and the consequence of this choice. For example,

–What occurs when we're out of touch with a friend over a period of time?

–Does the saying, "out of sight, out of mind," have an application here?

– What rules would people live by if there was no heavenly rule to Influence them?

–Name some differences between a constitutional Rule of Law and the Rule of God?

–Is keeping the Sabbath really that important? What about those, now Struck down, and out of style, so-called Blue Laws?

–Is there a conflict between the Ten Commandments and the U.S. Constitution?

–If there is a conflict, what can be done about it?

–Should Christians and the Church become involved in such a conflict?

–Would being involved in such a conflict be religious, social, or political?

–Where does the right of one person begin and another person end?

–How should Christians engage themselves when applying God's love in such matters?

The point is, although we can choose the right God and focus our attention on God, and regardless how meticulous we might be with our language and our behavior, it is imperative that we remain in constant touch with Him lest we forget, neglect, or abandon his providential love and care. God's words from the mountain were delivered to Moses and the Hebrew children as rules for their living Godly lives.

These rules for both their individual and corporate conduct were strengthened by requiring that the Hebrew people "Remember the Sabbath Day, to keep it holy." God expects no less from us, so...

"Stay in Touch!"

CHAPTER 6.

ESTABLISH GOOD BONDS OF BELONGING

"Honor your father and your mother..."
—Exodus 20:12

The Fifth Commandment is about developing good bonds of belonging, and this begins at home. First, we were not created to live in isolation; we were created for a relationship with one another. There is something within each of us that yearns to belong, to be accepted and appreciated, to be needed, to contribute something of ourselves in the building of community, and to be justifiably blessed or rewarded for our efforts. Second, the home is the first classroom where the lessons in human relationships are learned. If we cannot get along with people in our home, we shouldn't be surprised if we have trouble with people outside our home. Third, if we cannot find community within the home, we'll seek to find community somewhere else. Therefore, our future is defined by the kind of community we associate with and help to construct. Our bonds of belonging begin at home, with our father and mother, but those bonds of belonging never end there.

The Fifth Commandment means that children must learn to respect and honor their parents, newly weds must continue to respect and honor their parents, middle-aged persons whose parents have grown old must still respect and honor them, and parents are to be respected and honored until they go to their graves and, even after one's parents have died, they are still to be remembered, respected and honored. Honoring our parents is a spiritually inherited duty which must be fulfilled from the cradle to the grave, and the implications of this Fifth Commandment extend far beyond the nuclear family of our childhood.

But, it should be pointed out, God's words from the mountain are first and foremost for our own benefit, *"..that we may live long and that it may go well with you."* This is part of the law of proportional return, which is also found elsewhere in the Scriptures as, for example: "cast your bread upon the waters and it shall return to you;" "with what measure you mete, it will be meted to you again;" and "whatsoever a man sows, that shall he also reap."

For all who choose to faithfully worship and serve the Lord our God, the attitude and feelings we bear toward our father and mother, more than anything else, lays the foundation for our attitude, ambitions, and code of conduct inherent for successful and meaningful bonds of belonging within the human community.

LaSuer and Sells, in Bonds of Belonging, point out, *"As the global village shrinks and we are drawn closer to each other, we are awakened to the pressing need to belong and care for each other."* With this in mind, we realize that we actually belong to a wide variety of family groupings. The local church to which we belong is certainly a family. The denomination of which our local church is a vital part is a larger family to which we belong. The same can be said of sororities and fraternal groups, as well as service clubs and volunteer organizations. Many corporations in which people are employed impress upon its employees this family connection. In one sense, the community, state, and country in which we reside is a family affair. There certainly is a need to recognize that all the world's people, in reality, is one great human family. Although some of these family connections may be close and personal while others may seem remote and indifferent, at the core of every human being is the gnawing desire to be wanted, to be accepted, to be needed, to feel secure, to be recognized, and to be rewarded.

It is recognized there are parents whose behavior places their children at risk, causing every sort of antisocial behavior to grow within them. And there is within every family grouping those whose life styles are so far outside the bounds of human dignity it befuddles the mind to see how they could ever be appreciated and respected. It is a given fact that there are persons within every family grouping who cause other members of the family endless grief and pain. It is this breakdown of the ideal with which we must all contend, but lowering the ideal is the wrong solution and only acerbates and compounds the problem. God's words from the mountain sets us on the road to recovery from that which would rob us of our own dignity, therefore, it is essential in our bonds of belonging for us to receive and develop the gift of seeing within others more than they see within themselves. It is simply believing that, within the eyes of God, our parents, and others, are more important than the wrong within their lives.

Therefore, the Fifth Commandment is the school for our bonds of belonging.

>*–It teaches us about our being loved, wanted and needed.*
>*–It teaches us about feeling safe and being appreciated.*
>*–It teaches us about trust and being entrusted.*
>*–It teaches us about community and our place within it.*
>*–It teaches us about responsibility and being worthwhile persons.*

—It teaches us about authority and obedience to the rules of living.
—It teaches us about noble human values and ambitions.
—It teaches us about compassion and understanding.
—It teaches us about truth, honor, and a sense of good judgment.
—It teaches us about respect for others and the world around us.
—It lays the groundwork for who we are and who we can choose to become.

And, The Fifth Commandment is the gateway to fulfilling the remaining commandments because, in fulfilling our relationship with the Lord our God...

—we learn to revere and bless (5th Commandment);
—we learn to control our feelings (6th Commandment);
—we learn respect for others (7th Commandment);
—we learn responsibility (8th Commandment);
—we learn to be truthful (9th Commandment);
—we learn that honor is more enduring than envy (10th Commandment).

Honoring of your father and mother begins a process for us to develop, strengthen and...

"Establish Good Bonds of Belonging."

CHAPTER 7.

CONTROL YOUR EMOTIONS

"You shall not murder..."
—Exodus 20:13

The histology and psychology of murder is that, ever since that day when Cane slew his brother, Able, murder has become one method of attempting to satisfy the discord of the human heart. It must be recognized, however, that every act of murder claims two victims: the one doing the murder and the one being murdered, because the act of murder separates both victims from a normal association with the rest of society; with one being buried and the other ending up outside the law of God and man.

The motives for commission of murder is as varied as the act itself, including hate, envy, jealousy, spite, revenge, suspicion, fear, lunacy, misguided-love, power, and profit. These motives for murder are listed in the Bible as "sin, therefore, sin is the real motive for murder. To harbor one of these motives, even for a moment, makes any person liable to the act of murder. Therefore, every effort to refrain from committing the act of murder must begin with a refrain from unduly entertaining any sin which would lead one to the actual act of murder.

The formula for controlling these destructive human emotions is to replace those motives with something far better.

The moral implications of the 6th Commandment, "You shall not murder," are horribly, tragically, and pitifully written in blazing news headlines and stamped on grieving hearts, bearing evidence that what may have began as simple sin has festered into an abominable act of human degradation; a ruthless, ungodly replacement for compassionate, noble human behavior. Simply stated, murder is a result of choosing the wrong god; of making wrong choices, and embracing wrong religious beliefs. Only one who pretends to be a god would ever sanction murder or the killing of another person in the name of a religion. Such a god is counterfeit, their religion is false, and their prophets are fraudulent.

There is, however, a Godly and spiritual response to this deadly disease to the human heart. *A'gape* (Godly love) is the opposite of *Evil*, and *doing good* is the opposite of *harboring sin.* The harboring of sin (or sinful thought) until it ferments into an evil act (murder) are but one and the same, having progressed from a beginning to a destructive conclusion.

Standing directly opposite of sin and evil, however, *A'gape* and *doing good* form a rich mixture of peace and joy conducive for abundant living. *A'gape* and *doing good* promotes happiness and life; *sin* and *evil* produces destruction and death. *A'gape* and *doing good* is a Godly and spiritual response to sin and its consequential death.

A'gape and doing good replaces hatred with acceptance, envy and jealously with understanding, spite and revenge with kindness and grace, suspicion and fear with patience and faith, lunacy with good judgment and a sound mind, misguided-love with prudence and temperance, and power and profit with humility and caring. A'gape and doing good always manages to be bigger than the situation and better than the problem.

A'gape and doing good follows the advice of Jesus. He said, love your enemies; turn the other cheek; overcome evil with good; if anyone requires you to carry his pack one mile, go two miles; love the Lord your God with all your heart and love your neighbor as yourself.

Therefore, strive to see everything through the eyes of God. Living daily in a whirl of "I," "Me," and "Mine" can be dangerous for the soul. In living such a life we quickly establish a routine of seeing things the way we want to see them, leading people into believing that evil is actually good. Consequently we endeavor to make everything conform with our perception of how we are led to believe that things should be. Like spoiled children (brats) we forget there is a *Higher Power* who just might happen to see things differently, and infinitely better, than we can.

To avoid the temptation which leads to sin, evil, murder, and death we should cultivate and benefit from the practice of seeing everything through the eyes of God by asking ourselves one of these simple questions:

–What is more important, the person or their attitude?
–What is more important, the person or their behavior?
–What is more important, the person or their background?
–What is more important, the person or their ineptness?
–What is more important, the person or their ability?
–What is more important, the person or the profit?

When we make such an inquiry, up front, we discover how quickly is dispersed the lurking sin which would have us slipping down some path where God never intended for us to travel.

There are, however, those who advocate that there is a difference between murder and killing. Many passages in the Old Testament provide cause in certain circumstances which permit the killing of another. The act of defense against attack from an enemy seems justifiable. The accidental cause of the death of a person hardly meets the definition of murder. And, the New Testament is surprisingly quiet about the whole matter, except Jesus says, "You have heard that it was said to the people long ago, 'Do not murder...but I tell you anyone who is angry with his brother will be subject to the judgment" (Matthew 5:21). Jesus also shuns the behavior of retaliatory action (Matthew 5:38-42), and tells us to "..love your enemies (Matthew 5:43-45).

The seventh commandment, however, speaks only of murder, which is the decision to take the life of another. This chapter foregoes an open discussion about killing, or any possible justification for killing. This chapter has endeavored instead to throw light upon the sin and evil which willingly takes control of the human heart, which in-the-end leads to the murder of another person, and in their place urges us to engage ourselves in practicing a more worthy view of others. The Lord urges you to accept, forgive, esteem, respect, honor, dignify, and praise others if you would...

"Control Your Emotions"

CHAPTER 8.

GOVERN YOUR PASSIONS

"You shall not commit adultery..."
—Exodus 20:14

When we were created by God, we were gifted with life and two wonderful and fulfilling appetites, the first of which was *hunger,* that we might eat and sustain life. The second was *sex,* that we might reproduce and replace ourselves. These gifts were of divine origin and designed for a divine wholeness within ourselves. The first man and woman satisfied these gifts with principled restraint and acceptable consummation until they crossed the boundary of proscribed behavior. Their subsequent decision to choose fruit from a forbidden tree brought upon them shame and a spiritual sickness called sin. These divine, sustaining appetites then became in them dangerous and destructive urges.

In regard to this second appetite, as often is the case, love was changed to lust, the means of procreation became a selfish passion of earthly pleasure, and the intimate realm of their being was corrupted. The ensuing result was that, unchecked, lust shattered and fragmented their human spiritual and physical wholeness. This continues to be a major source of our human dilemma.

Since the gift of human sexuality was meant by God to be a wonderful and fulfilling gift, intended for divine purposes, the obvious question is, "If sex was intended to be a wonderful gift, why have we made it so ugly?" Since everything God created was blessed and holy, how has sex became such a problem for society? How has this wonderful and purposeful gift become for much of humanity an enigma of shame, degradation, and even death? The truth is, it is the misapplication of this gift that shames and destroys those who choose to misappropriate it for selfish and personal pleasure is a behavioral practice that is not sanctioned by God.

The Hebrew word for adultery is *na'aph* (naw-af), meaning *to commit adultery, to apostatize, adulterer(ess),* and *woman that breaketh wedlock*. Another Hebrew word of the same root is *na'atis* (pronounced naw-ats'), meaning to *scorn, abhor, despise, (give occasion to) blaspheme,* and *to greatly provoke.* The Hebrew text in Exodus 21:14 is: You shall not *na'aph, which is interpreted* to mean, "You shall not commit adultery."

While the Hebrew word *na-aph* is translated at one point, *"woman that breaketh wedlock,"* the prohibition is generic because the Hebrew *na* implies *any breathing thing,* thus any breathing male or female would be equally inclusive to the prohibition.

To apostatize or *to be an apostate* means to be one who denies or turns against the covenant with God; to become a defector, a deserter, a heretic. Since man and woman were created by God to bear his image, the breaking or breaching of a covenant (such as marriage) between two persons is tantamount to breaking a covenant with their creator. In other words, as individual persons, we are still part of the whole and to disrupt even one part is to, with rippling effect, disrupt the whole.

In creation, human beings were also given the extraordinary gift of "feelings" (emotions, passions, beliefs, ideas, sense of self-esteem, etc.). The commission of adultery, therefore, not only tramples a covenant made between persons, its commission also provokes human "feelings," not only of the parties involved, but of society as a whole. Ultimately, our misuse of sex is a provocation of God.

Also, since sex is the gift by which humans might reproduce and replace themselves with offspring, the conceiving and siring of children outside the covenant of marriage places those children at great risk regarding: first, themselves as sacred individuals; second, the fabric of a well-ordered society; and third, the well-being of a holy creation. Thus, adultery turns what was meant to be a wonderful and holy gift into a splintering, dividing, and conquering evil whose final verdict becomes ruination and doom.

My long-standing definition of marriage provided for prospective brides and grooms has been, *"a marriage is a ministry of two people to each other."* There is no other venue in which ministry can be more basic, or appropriate, than in the bonds of marriage, where each partner tenderly attend the needs of one another.

This ministry carried out between two persons includes acceptance, approval, understanding, protection, esteem, encouragement, and appreciation. When this kind of ministry is enjoined between two persons, there exists a recognition between them that each partner is important, and the need to receive or provide such ministry elsewhere is removed. Incidentally, it is my contention there is no such thing as "a marriage problem." Rather, any problem within the bonds of marriage always boils down to a "people problem" on the part of either one marriage partner, or both. Usually, this occurs when one or both of the partners cease to minister to their partner, or one partner's conduct and behavior becomes so egregious that a healing ministry becomes no longer possible.

The Seventh Commandment, however, is more than a stern prohibition against misappropriation of a wonderful gift. It also goes beyond the usage of that holy means of reproducing and replacing human life. Its placement here goes to the heart of our relationship with God, and with our human family. Both relationships are equally important to our Lord and they are essential for our well-being.

The misappropriation of sex, from the first generation of creation to modern times, is merely another sign of people making wrong choices; of disallowing the opportunity to overcome evil with good. Keeping this wonderful and fulfilling gift in holy covenant with our Creator is another means of fulfilling the very First Commandment of choosing the right God.

Again, there are those in every generation who have attempted to change this written in stone commandment. The so-called sexual revolution of the sixties and seventies did not bring us into the age of enlightenment but was, merely, another attempt to discredit and dislodge the influence of the true and living God whose words from the mountain are the only road map with the correct directions for arriving safely home.

The person who commits adultery may temporarily satisfy their personal lust, but adultery degrades the bond of marriage, debases both self and the other person, destroys community, and sins against God's holiness. Those who misappropriate this gift of God are never justified in their behavior or lifestyle. However, their greatest shame, their greatest sin, and their greatest condemnation, arises from the harm they inflict against another person's spiritual and physical well-being. Their greatest failure is to wantonly disregard another person as someone of sacred worth; as someone to be esteemed, cherished, and protected instead of being debased. And, mutual agreement between two consenting adults does nothing to change the nature of this sin.

The truth is, no one justifies the sexual rapist, the sexual abuser, the sexual exploiter, or the sexual pedophile. These activities were never justified in the beginning, neither can they be justified as "normal" activity in this day and time. Now, any activity may be rationalized, even murder, but every attempt to rationalize the carrying out of a sinful proclivity always falls short of a truthful biblical justification. It is not the proclivity itself that is sinful; sin lies in the activity which carries out that proclivity. This is the broader understanding of Jesus' teaching: *"What goes into a man's mouth does not make him 'unclean,' but what comes out of his mouth, that is what makes him 'unclean'"* (Matthew 15:11). In other words, we cannot have it both ways. The choice is always: God's way, or the wrong way.

The truth is, from the dawn of creation, "people are important," and God's words from the mountain have been clearly laid out in a series of steps for our acceptance and guidance. Choose the right God, stay focused on God, and keep it clean. Next, stay in touch with God and cherish your bonds of belonging. Then follows some important directives designed for us to constantly ratify so that we may reinforce our initial choosing of the right God; by first choosing to control our powerful emotions, then choosing to honor, respect and champion the spiritual well-being of others.

Christ clearly taught that in the scheme of all things, people are important and everything else is secondary. Therefore, establish your relationship with people by recognizing that they are holy, recognizing that they were created in the image of God who, from the beginning, gifted their holy creation worthy of his eternal love and grace. In this regard:

—*choose to honor and respect others; do not debase another for your own selfish gain, pleasure, or purposes.*

—*choose to honor and respect yourself; do not debase yourself in the eyes of God or your neighbor.*

—*choose to honor and respect the marriage covenant; it is one of the Cornerstones for human society.*

—*choose to honor and strengthen others. That strengthens the entire family of God.*

—*choose to honor God; do not be an apostate (one who is a defector, a deserter, a heretic). Do not choose to be a na'aph (naw-af), an adulterer(ess). And do not choose behavior which provokes another to wrath.*

The bottom line is this, we can choose to honor God by choosing to be charitable and considerate, loving and serving. These choices are more than refraining from some particular act, rather it is the wisdom of always choosing the more noble behavior because we believe that, next to God, people are important and everything else is secondary. Therefore...

"Govern Your Passions."

CHAPTER 9.

PROTECT YOUR REPUTATION

"You shall not steal..."
—Exodus 20:15

Having possession of any thing, item, or asset carries with it certain reasonable responsibilities by the possessor. There is also a reasonable expectation regarding that possession by all other persons. It is important, therefore, that we view the holding and use of possessions from both the position of the divine and that of an ordered society.

The first view is from the position of the Divine.

> —all things were created by God and belong to him, not to us.
> —it pleases God to bestow certain gifts upon us and we are expected to be good stewards of all God's gifts, namely, air, water, earth, and sky are both given to us and loaned to us for proper use and for safekeeping.
> --our bodies and souls are both given to us and loaned to us for safe-keeping.

–the earth and all its natural elements, beasts, birds, fish, and peoples are either for our use or loaned to us for our good stewardship and our safekeeping.

–from the position of the Divine, it is important for us to comprehend that the distinction between those gifts we are given permission to use and those *we must not misappropriate* as our own. *To misappropriate any gift from God is, in effect, to steal from God.*

–we see this theological position reflected in the Hebrew's offering of first fruits to God.

–the act of thanksgiving recognizes that all created things and beings, first, belong to God. We are caretakers, or stewards of God's creation.

The second view is from the position of an ordered society.

–early societies organized themselves into governments with fixed laws and rulers (Judges).

–earliest governments recognized the individual and community right for the ownership of gifts, including self, family, land, ideas, property, assets, etc.

–when any individual, family, or community moved into an unclaimed and uninhabited land, such was considered a gift and was not to be usurped or taken by another. The land could be given away, loaned, leased, or sold, but the land was considered as "possessed,"or owned, and was not to be usurped or misappropriated by another.

–That possession was to be protected by its owner(s) who held it as a gift for safekeeping, however, the possession could be sold or traded to another "possessor."

–when any person discovered a ruby, gold, or anything precious which was not possessed by another it was a found gift which could be claimed and the same rules applied.

–when anyone planted an olive tree on their owned land, it was a possession earned, and the same rules applied.

The long and the short is, *Everything belongs to somebody.* This general rule was applied in ancient days. It also applies today. Everything is either possessed or not possessed, but if it is not a gift or you have not rightfully obtained it, it's not yours. An "act of stealing" means to appropriate property in the care of another person without proper permission. This word from the mountain implies that everything belongs to somebody, somewhere, and this Eighth Commandment clearly means that, *"if it's not yours, don't pick it up without permission of the owner."* To misappropriate anything for your own that is possessed by another is an act of stealing, betrays God's words from the mountain, and rips asunder the fabric of an ordered society.

More important than being a prohibition, however, this 8th Commandment concerns the right of ownership; the right to obtain and possess property, and the responsibility for its safekeeping and good stewardship.

In reality, your worth as a person is identified by your reputation; a bond held sacred by those who know you, both as a person of honor and honesty and as a good steward in the sight of God and your neighbor. Therefore, zealously...

"Protect Your Reputation."

CHAPTER 10.

BE TRUTHFUL

"You shall not give false testimony...."
—Exodus 20:16

F. Scott wrote: *"O what a tangled web we weave when first we practice to deceive...."* That adage speaks volumes in behalf of the Ninth Commandment.

Christ was crucified by lies before he died on a cross. Surrounded by his accusers that dark night, he stood alone, without friends to support him. Those present were primarily those who had falsified reports, made irresponsible charges, and borne false witness against him. Hours later he hung limply under a hot Palestinian sky. He was dead, but through the centuries the cross has remained not only a beautiful symbol of God's redeeming love, but at the same time a gruesome and ghastly reminder of man's inhumanity against his fellow human beings.

The Ninth Commandment was given by God to preserve the truth. In the case of Christ, however, there were: first, those who twisted the truth and substituted in truth's place, false reports, absurd rumors, and outright lies and, second, those who cowered in fear of the authorities and failed to speak out in Christ's behalf.

There are six basic ways to trample upon, smear, and debase the truth.

1. Truth Can Be Twisted.
   – one must be careful to distinguish between facts and opinions, or fiction.
   – an assassination of the truth is to declare as fact a partial truth which in all honesty is merely an interpretation or impression.
   – one must handle carefully what one hears, reads, and sees.
   – one must be careful, therefore, with opinions, judgments, and gossip.

2. Truth Can Be Ignored
   – we can license a lie by letting it go unchallenged (confront lies with love).
   – truth is never a danger, but lies can grow until they ruin everything and everyone they touch.

3. Truth Can Be Rationalized
   – we rationalize truth when we attempt to absolve or justify bigotry, protect wrongdoing, defend bad judgment, vindicate obscenity, or exonerate evil.
   – one can also rationalize and discredit truth by deliberately underrating or discounting another person; either their worth or their ability.

4. Truth Can Be Suppressed
   – Nazism, Communism, Secularism, Humanism, Terrorism, and fanatical religions are among those who have suppressed truth.

–Stonewalling, coverups, or hiding the truth never serves the higher good.

–also see Romans 1:18-32

5. Truth Can Be Exaggerated. This falls into two categories:
   (1) one kind of exaggeration uses enthusiasm and superlatives to have a desired effect. This kind of exaggeration is usually harmless, i.e. sports fans chanting , "We're #1."
   (2) the other kind or exaggerated truth recklessly uses extremes to skew the facts, i.e. "He's <u>never</u> been on time," or "they're <u>all </u>against me."

6. <u>Truth Can Be Violated By Insinuation</u>

   i.e., when one person says to another, "Oh, you haven't met John? You <u>Will</u>!"

The spirit of truth recognizes the ugly untruth for what it is; a foundation for evil to work its curse; an enemy of righteousness; a perversion of justice; and an affront to God. Scott was correct when he wrote, *"O what a tangled web we weave when first we practice to deceive...."*

A high school girl attending her school's prom, spent the night at another girl's house, but had to be home early the following morning. Her boy friend picked her up from her friends house and drove her home at 6:15 A.M. In her excitement of preparing for the prom, she had forgotten to take a change of clothes with her. A neighborhood gossip saw her arrive home at 6:15 a.m., still dressed in her evening gown. Before the tongues quit wagging, the young girl's reputation had been ruined. In deep distress, she killed herself. There was a note to her mother saying that she did not understand, but somebody must have seen her arrival home at 6:15 that morning and assumed the worse. The neighbor, who was sitting nearby when the note was read aloud, muttered: "Oh, my God, I've killed her." In a sad way, the neighbor had!

Truth, like love, is defined by the motive of one's heart, mind, and soul. When we speak, and how we speak. The arrangement of words, their inflections and emphasis handle more than facts and figures. The lives and reputations of others, as well as our own, are held therein.

The reckless handling of truth, outright lying, gossip, and deceit spurred the Apostle Paul to write, "..speaking the truth in love, we will in all things grow up unto him who is the head, that is, Christ. (Ephesians 4:15). So...

"Be Truthful!"

CHAPTER 11.

HARNESS YOUR DESIRES

"You shall not covet..."
—Exodus 20:17

What is it that drives the human psyche to gather, to accumulate, to possess, to achieve, or to imagine that the grass just beyond one's immediate grasp is somehow greener and somewhat better? Everyone has heard the warning: "All that glitters is not gold." Still, just in case, people keep their gold pans handy.

The 10th Commandment challenges the lure of materialism and, in its place, beckons people to embrace a quest for spirituality in its place. Christ challenged us to place "spirituality" at the forefront of our yearning hearts when he said:

"Do not be so concerned about your house and clothes...but seek first the kingdom of God and his righteousness..." (Matthew 6:25-33).

The Tenth Commandment is God's summary statement. These concluding words spoken to Moses from the mountain pulls together all that's gone before; establishing a sharp contrast between a life of selfishness that seeks materialism, and that of a life that finds satisfaction in the spirituality of a relationship with God and humankind. One kind of life is about getting and protecting to the point of war, and is set against a life that is about being, relating in love, and the provisions of peace.

Coveting, avarice and greed leave a hole within us which cannot be filled and a hunger which can never be fully satisfied.

From Matthew 6:25-33, we find that man is not born for materialism, but for immortality; he is not born for sectarianism, but for fellowship; and he is not born for divisions and differences, but for love. Shortly before his arrest and crucifixion, Christ said to his disciples: "I would that my joy might be in you and that your joy might be complete" (John 15:11). He also said: "Peace I leave with you, my peace I give to you: not as the world gives do I give to you. Let not your heart be troubled, neither let it be afraid" (John 14:27). God intended for his people to live lives filled with joy, peace, and happiness.

This is not a popular view to those salesmen on Madison Avenue who would have us believe that joy, peace, and happiness is something you can buy by purchasing the right product, by living in the correct house, or driving a certain car, wearing the right clothes, using the elegant cosmetic, serving the right whiskey, etc.

This is mockery, because "things" do not satisfy the deep inner urges of the human heart. Material things can neither satisfy the spirit of mankind nor the Spirit of God. To begin with, "things" are temporal; they rust, wear out, burn out, break, or go out of style, which leads us to conclude:

1. Material things make absolutely no contribution to immortality.

   Because we were born as eternal beings, materialism cannot help but leave us empty for something else. We were born to be filled with the goodness of God.

2. Material things cannot satisfy. Because they are, by nature, tyrannical, Things tend to bind and imprison us. We were born to be free.

3. Material things bore us because "things", of themselves are dead.

   Materialism does not talk, laugh, or love. We were born for living relationships.

Conclusion: What is the purpose of the 10th Commandment? The Apostle Paul established a criteria for his self which we would do well to embrace as our standard for a well-controlled lifestyle.

"...I have learned to be content whatever the circumstances. I know that it is to be in need, and I know what it is to have plenty. I have learned the secret of being content in any and every situation, whether well fed or hungry, whether living in plenty or in want. I can do everything through him who gives me strength." –Philippians 4:11-13.

Our egocentric desires must be challenged and subdued from over stepping the boundaries of shared love and mutual respect. Our ego massaging wants must not stray from our genuine needs because it's a false illusion that makes us think the grass some place else is a little greener than the grass in our own backyard. Therefore,

"Harness Your Desires!"

CHAPTER 12.

───────────── ⚬ ⚭ ⚬ ─────────────

BE BLESSED, AND BE A BLESSING

God first spoke to Moses upon the heights of Mount Horeb, when he sent Moses back to Egypt to deliver the Hebrew people from their life of human bondage.

Then God spoke to Moses a second time on Mount Sinai, and the Hebrew people were guided for the next 1300 years by the Ten Commandments which God provided them at his second meeting with Moses.

After this period of time, a time when there was deliverance, a homeland, a rule of Judges and Kings, the Hebrew people were again subjected to the rule of others.

There was a need for additional words from God, and these were delivered by God's Son on the Mount of Beatitudes.

This is a look at some of those additional words called, *The Beatitudes.*

"Now when he saw the crowds, he went up on a mountain and sat down. His disciples came to him, and he began to teach them, saying: 'Blessed are the poor in spirit, for theirs is the kingdom of heaven. Blessed are those who mourn, for they will be comforted. Blessed are the meek, for they will inherit the earth. Blessed are those who hunger and thirst for righteousness, for they will be filled. Blessed are the merciful, for they will be shown mercy. Blessed are the pure in heart, for they will see God. Blessed are the peacemakers, for they will be called sons of God. Blessed are those who are persecuted because of righteousness, for theirs is the kingdom of heaven..." –Matthew 5:1-10

The Beatitudes are eight statements given by Jesus concerning the virtues of human life. These are other important words from the mountain. These words are spoken from a different mountain, but the beatitudes are as important as the words spoken to Moses on Mount Sinai. The beatitudes are simply stated, but have profound meaning. Like a road map for living, they are directives by which we can successfully govern our lives. They guide. They point. They teach. They show us those values about which God deeply cares and desires that we wholly embrace.

The first Beatitude is, *"Blessed are the poor in spirit..."* This beatitude is the linchpin for all the other seven beatitudes. Just as *choosing the right God* is fundamental to fulfilling all the other commandments, so is the first beatitude basic to fulfilling all the other beatitudes. If we fail to grasp the depth and fulfill the meaning of this first beatitude the others, by themselves, have an unstable foundation.

The Greek word for *poor* is *"ptochos,"* and means to have nothing and to be completely empty. This does not mean to be in poverty from lack of worldly goods, for there is no blessing in that kind of poverty. It means that the poor in spirit are we who realize there are no spiritual means within ourselves for attaining salvation. The poor in spirit realize our salvation is wholly dependent upon the grace of God.

Therefore, the poor in spirit are not self-assertive, self-reliant, self-confident, self-centered, self-sufficient, or self-esteeming. The poor in spirit realize that our salvation cannot depend on our own given characteristics of birth, family, position, wealth, race, nationality, culture, physiology, education, career, talents, abilities, etc. None of that matters. The poor in spirit are conscious of our sinful nature, knowing in our hearts we are completely unworthy of the grace poured upon us by a loving, forgiving, redeeming, and holy God.

While the *poor in spirit* realize there is nothing we can do or say in our own behalf that would justify us to be in the presence of God, we recognize that, through belief, repentance and faith, God's love descends from beyond to transform, justify, and declare us worthy. Henceforth, God accepts us in spite of our shortcomings because God's grace deems us more important than our sinful nature. God has himself acted in our behalf, has offered us a way to salvation, and has given us a promise, all of which is sealed by the suffering and death of Christ. All we now must do is believe God's promise, accept God's offer, and become involved as God's servants.

In the death of Christ, who on Calvary's Cross took our place and bore unto himself the punishment we deserved, all who realize there is no means of salvation save through Christ's suffering and death, are forgiven and pardoned through God's wondrous sacrificial gift of love. Therefore, *"blessed are the poor in spirit..."*

The second Beatitude is, *"Blessed are those who mourn..."* The Greek word for *mourn* is *"pentheo,"* which means to grieve. We grieve, first, because of our sinful nature and, secondly, we grieve because of the sin and evil which enslaves others. Realizing that sin and evil greatly hurts and causes grief to our heavenly Father, the believer grieves for the pain which is inflicted upon God. And, we who grieve because of our Father's pain, are spiritually comforted with an abiding faith that the time of anguish will soon end, coupled with a steadfast hope those who now grieve the Father's heart will come to their senses and also be transformed.

First, we receive a good measure of spiritual comfort from our own transformed relationship with God, a spiritual comfort that is experienced both here and also in the hereafter, when our comfort is to be more completely consummated. Our immediate spiritual comfort is knowing that we are in a wholesome relationship with God; when unbelief is replaced with faith, sin is replaced with forgiveness, shame is replaced with acceptance, rebellion is replaced with love, and darkness is replaced with light. There is comfort in knowing that, in Christ, we are a new creation.

Second, believers grieve because of the sin which grips and enslaves others. We care that people hurt, but at the same time we realize things could be different. We grieve because the evil and sin dwelling within others imparts such a great havoc upon the people of earth, an anguish that is neither necessary nor profitable. The believer joins with the Father in grieving for those who stand apart and against both the Father and the Father's own children. However, the believer sees from afar that glorious day when this warfare will be ended and the swords of destruction shall be beat into plowshares of peace; when the people of earth will fall in love again. Therefore, *"blessed are those who mourn..."*

The third Beatitude is, *"Blessed are the meek..."* The Greek word for *meek* is *"praus,"* and means those who have been broken and domesticated. The meek are neither wishy-washy nor shy, but they are tamed from their pride, arrogance, and vanity, that they may do their Father's will; much like oxen are broken and disciplined to the yoke and plow. The meek recognize their Master and are obedient to him, much like sheep who recognize and obey their Master's voice.

The meek know God, and they see the presence of God in everything. Not one thing on earth or in heaven is too vast and nothing is too small to ignore the significance of God's mighty presence therein. Like Moses, the believer sees the presence of God in every burning bush and they hear his words from the mountain saying anew, *"I Am Who I Am."* This spiritual insight is no small thing. It is not for weaklings, doubters, deniers, or destroyers. Being meek means being courageous enough to believe, bold enough to comply, gallant enough to serve with valor, yet patient enough to inherit the earth. Therefore, *"blessed are the meek..."*

The fourth Beatitude is, *"Blessed are they who hunger and thirst for righteousness..."* The Greek word for *hunger* is *"peiaro,"* meaning to famish or crave in a pinching manner, and comes from the root word *"penes,"* which means to toil for daily bread. Hunger, or *"peiaro,"* is a squeezed craving. The Greek word for *thirst* is *"dipsao,"* which means to thirst for. The word *Righteousness* is a translation from the Greek word *"dikaiosune,"* which means equity of character, and comes from the root word *"dikaios"* which means, by implication, to be innocent or holy. The fourth beatitude can be said to mean that "blessed are they who have within their souls a squeezed or compressed craving and thirst for holy justice; first, for oneself and, second, for creation in general. It is a burning desire to be in complete accord with that which is right, just, and holy and it includes those things that are virtuous, noble, pure, morally upright, and ethically spotless in the sight of God.

Those believers who hunger and thirst for righteousness not only believe and practice such, but see by faith that coming day of the Lord when "justice will roll on like a river, righteousness like a never-failing stream" (Amos 5:24). The righteous see by faith that coming day when all sin and evil will exist no more. Therefore, *"Blessed are those who hunger and thirst for righteousness..."*

The fifth Beatitude is, *"Blessed are the merciful..."* The Greek word for *merciful* is *"eleemon,"* meaning to be merciful; or compassionate. Those who are merciful not only feel within their souls the pain and suffering of the poor, the lonely, the outcast, the abused, and the lost; they possess a Godly desire to alleviate both the pain and the cause of suffering, and they give of themselves to that great cause. The merciful desire to comfort the afflicted as they themselves have been comforted in the times of their own distress.

The mercy provided by believers is given with readiness and gladness, affection and tenderness, forgiveness and healing, and this mercy is more than random acts of charity; it is a deliberately chosen way of life bestowed in tribute to the One who first loved and conferred mercy on us. Therefore, our ministry of mercy is not restricted only to those of our own household, but to strangers and the outcasts of society, realizing that when mercy is given to the least of these we are rendering mercy to Christ (Matthew 25:40).

Because God loves us, forgives and accepts us, heals and restores us, and empowers us in a brand-new way, believers manifest their newly given Godliness by sharing with others that which we have received. It has been said that a blessing is not a blessing until it has been shared. Some have said that mercy is like one beggar, finding bread, then hastens to inform other beggars where they can find bread. Therefore, *"Blessed are the merciful..."*

The sixth Beatitude is, *"Blessed are the pure in heart..."* The Greek word for *pure* is *"katharos,"* meaning clean, clear, or pure. The Greek word for *heart* is *"Kardia,"* meaning the heart of, or middle of. Figuratively, it refers to the core of one's thoughts or feelings, as the core of one's mind. Thus, in order to be blessed, among other characteristics one must possess at the core of one's being a mind of clean and clear thoughts and feelings concerning God and the living of their lives in a manner which pleases God and his Christ.

Because of our inherent sinful nature, our daily thoughts are rife with temptations to do evil; lust, fornication, thievery, envy, greed, arrogance, deceit, slander, foolishness, murder, etc. Part and partial to the spiritual transformation of our nature, wherein God forgives, accepts, heals, cleanses, and restores; God also gives us spiritual power to resist and overcome future temptations to do evil. The temptations will return again and again, but a clean heart will not succumb or give root to the enticements of Satan. After Christ overcame Satan's temptations in the wilderness, Satan left Christ until an opportune time (Luke 4:13). Christ said that it is not the temptation, but the act of evil which defiles a person (Mark 7:15).

The pure in heart are those who look to God for strength to resist temptation and evil. We have no such strength of resistance within ourselves but, to maintain a clean heart, God constantly makes available to us his spiritual presence, which presence is more potent than that of Satan. We are not left to fend for ourselves against the lures of Satan; the Spirit of God is with us.*"Blessed are the pure in heart..."*

The seventh Beatitude is, *"Blessed are the peacemakers..."* The Greek word,*"eirenopoios,"* is interpreted *peacemaker* and comes from a root word, *iraynay,"* which means: as one, peace, quietness, or rest that sets at one again. Figuratively, it means to unite that which has been broken or to make whole again those who are in discord. It includes all who have been at war with God, who have been at war with others and, also, all who have been at war with God, all who oppose the kingdom of God, and all who are divided from one another.

The peacemakers are those who have ceased their opposition to God and have themselves been reconciled to God and to the reign of God's kingdom. However, the peacemakers not only espouse and preserve peace between ourselves and God, but we take up God's cause to end all enmity and strife with which others constantly wage war against the reign of God. Thus, peacemakers are advocates who call upon others to make peace with God and champions who endeavor to call all the people of earth to gather at the table of reconciliation that we might become one again; one with God and one with one another.

This yearning for reconciliation and oneness was urgently expressed by Christ as he prayed in the garden of Gethsemane: *"My prayer is not for them alone. I pray also for those who believe in me through their message, that all of them may be one, Father, just as you are in me and I am in you. May they also be in us so that the world may believe that you have sent me. I have given them the glory that you gave me, that they may be one as we are one; I in them you in me. May they be brought to complete unity to let the world know that you sent me and have loved them even as you loved me..." (John 17:23).*

Peacemakers may abhor sin and evil, but they love unity because they love the Lord and they love people; no exceptions. Peacemakers are those who, in faith and love, willingly infiltrate and fill the world's dens of iniquity with a plea for reconciliation and wholeness. Peacemakers see by faith that great day when all God's children shall become one again. *"Blessed are the peacemakers..."*

The eighth Beatitude is, *"Blessed are those who are persecuted because of righteousness..."* The Greek word *"dioko"* is here translated as persecuted, but it means to pursue or to be pursued, and given to as to suffer. It comes from the Greek verb, *"dio,"* which means to be timid (as to be faithless), or fearful.

First, the eighth beatitude is directed toward any person who is timid or faithless and treats the beatitudes like a smorgasbord from which to pick and choose some things while ignoring or discarding the other beatitudes. It is an all or nothing deal concerning righteousness which God's children are invited to embrace, and blessed are those who are ever faithful to the totality of righteousness.

Second, the eighth beatitude is also intended to bolster our faith, hope and righteousness when we are pursued and persecuted solely because we have embraced and espoused a life of righteousness. Whenever righteousness becomes a threat to sin and evil, that sin and evil in others make the righteous of God a handy target in their warfare against God and his holy kingdom. Christ was crucified, in part, because of indwelling evil in some. Why should the righteous followers of Christ expect better treatment? We are not always called to be martyrs but we are called to be faithful. It is by faith and by the power of God that victory over sin and death will ultimately prevail. That's the truth! *"Blessed are those who are persecuted because of righteousness..."*

Now, having chosen Christ over the ways of sin and evil, having been blessed with the transforming gift of God's righteousness, and having received instructions which honor the righteousness of God within our hearts, the followers of Christ are also taught what to do with God's blessings.

Christ assures us that we are God's salt of the earth and we are the light of the world (Matthew 5:13-14). We are first blessed, then we are sent forth as a blessing to others. We are not only accepted and included into God's kingdom, we are anointed and included in God's plan to reconcile those prodigals who are in rebellion against God. It is a calling which each generation must answer because each new generation must, itself, be rescued from their naturally sinful inclination.

It would seem that, since each new generation must be redeemed, Satan and evil already holds the upper hand and God's task is never ending. God's task is not, however, an impossible one. Any single generation within the cycle of birth and death can become wholly transformed and their offspring would inherit their righteous DNA with a holy nature, instead of continuing the corrupted nature of the old line that is prone to sin and evil. Think about it! Through one man, Adam, sin and death entered into the world, and his children inherited his corrupted DNA; but through the second Adam, Christ Jesus, righteousness becomes the transformed nature in those who are born again by his Spirit. Who knows? With God all things are possible.

These are those words from the mountain, spoken by Jesus. They, too, are the words of God, therefore, receive them, believe them, embrace them, and be blessed that you might...

Become a Blessing to Others in His Name!

CHAPTER 13.

BE SALT AND BE LIGHT

Now, having chosen Christ over the way of sin and evil, having been blessed with the living gift of God's righteousness, having received instruction for the maintenance of God righteousness within our hearts and for our journey as followers of Christ, we are now instructed about what to do with God's blessings.

We are to be God's salt of the earth, and we are to be God's light of the world. We are both blessed and we are sent forth to be a blessing to others. We are not only accepted and included into God's kingdom, we are commissioned and included in God's plan to reconcile all prodigals who remain in rebellion against God.

Christ's statement to his disciples, following the eight Beatitudes, is a forerunner of his Great Commission in Matthew 28:17b-20. Jesus said: *"All authority in heaven and on earth have been given to me. Therefore go and make disciples of all nations, baptizing them in the name of the Father, and of the Son, and of the Holy Spirit, and teaching them to obey everything I have commanded you. And surely I will be with you always, to the very end of the age."* Think about what Jesus is telling us in this scripture:

"All authority in heaven and on earth..." That is powerful stuff!

"Therefore go..." It's a commission! It's a directive! It's our marching orders!

"Make disciples of all nations..." Everyone is included! No one is excluded! Every person is to be a brother or a sister!

"Father, Son, and Holy Spirit..." We're not on our own! We're on a mission!
God has established a mission with broad boundaries! Not for ourselves! It's for God!

"Teaching them to obey everything I have commanded you..." Love God! and Love one another!

No arguments over mottos on coins, symbols on courthouses, or Christmas trees and manger scenes. That's trifling stuff which mostly misses the main point. God keeps telling us to, "Stop trying to defend me! I am quite capable of protecting myself! Just go! Proclaim me! That's your assignment. No trifling! No apologies! No excuses!"

"And surely I will be with you*..."* No comma! No conditions! It's a promise!

"You are the salt of the earth"

Here, Jesus takes a common element and turns it into an uncommon example of what his disciples are to be like.

First, salt may be a common element, but it carries a high price. So do we! The fact that Romans soldiers once received salt rations as part of their wages indicates the value of salt. In biblical times, salt was worth it's weight in gold. So are we!

Second, salt made a difference between life and death. So do we! People needed to eat in order to survive. We need food to fuel our bodies. Nourishment is essential for survival. Fats, proteins, and minerals help us function. But, most food is bland in taste. Without salt or something to make food tasty to the palate, we would eat less and deprive ourselves this needed nourishment. Therefore, salt helps our intake of essential nourishment as fuel for the body.

Third, salt preserves, cleanses, and saves. It's a preservative for meat and vegetables, as well as an agent against germs. It's intake also helps to conserve and hold water longer within the human body. In a hot and thirsty land, without water people quickly dehydrate and die.

What Jesus wants his disciples to understand is that these beatitudes which he has just handed them to embrace as *a way of life,* along with the Ten Commandments which God had previously given to Moses, are exactly what they needed, as well as being what all the people of earth need.

With these, they can make a difference. Without these, they are nothing. With them, they live; without them, they will surely die. So will we!

What Jesus is telling us then is this: I have made you like salt, but if you trash what I have given you, if you toss it away, or cast it on the sand under your feet, how can you gather it again as salt to preserve, cleanse, and save. It's only value then will be as something to walk on, but dying people don't walk very far.

"You are the light of the world"

Genesis, chapter 1, verse 3, says, following the creation of the heavens and the earth:

"...God said, "Let there be light," and there was light. God saw that the light was good, and he separated the light from the darkness..."

Thus begins a distinction between light and darkness, or day and night, and these two stark differences have, ever since, been employed to define that difference between good and evil; between what is holy and what is profane.

It is that distinction which prompted the prophet Isaiah, to write:

"The people walking in darkness have seen a great light; on those living in the land of the shadow of death, a light has shined"
(Isaiah 9:7).

In John, chapter 7, Jesus goes to the Feast of Tabernacles, which is also known as the Festival of Lights, a harvest festival held on 15th day of the seventh month. In the time of Christ it lasted for eight days.

It was the third of three principle Hebrew Feast Days, which included the festivals of Passover and Pentecost. It was to remind the Hebrews of their time of wandering in the desert, when a cloud of smoke had led them by day and a pillar of fire had guided them by night.

Booths, and long houses were constructed to permit entry of earliest morning rays. The Brazen Altar in the Temple was Illuminated when the door was opened. Central to the feast was the Ten Commandments, given as Light by God to Moses at Sinai, at the place where God had first appeared to him "as Light" in a burning bush.

During this Feast of Tabernacles, or Festival of Lights, Jesus was teaching in the Temple courts and told his listeners: *"I am the Light of the World. Whoever follows me will never walk in darkness, but will have the light of life."* –John 8:12

Physical Light helps us to <u>see</u> , but Spiritual Light helps us to <u>know</u>.

The application being made by Jesus is this:

–"I am the Light..." Whoever follows me will never walk in darkness (John 8:12).

–"You are the light of the world..." Let your light shine (Matthew 5:14).

–God is Light (the source). You are the Light (reflect it).

–A lantern with a dirty glass needs to be cleaned. Let the Light of Jesus shine through.

–Airport runway lights have a drawing power. They <u>pull</u> an airplane to safety.

–Let the light in you shine that others may see. Draw others to God.

Do not hide the light under a basket.

Do not be faithless, or timid, or fearful to manifest the light.

–Place your light on a stand so others around you may also see.

Be bold, be courageous, lift it up, hold it high, let others see.

–Let your good deeds be a shining witness to the love of God that is in you.

The Lord wants you, the world needs you, and you can make a world of difference to others. Therefore,

Be Salt and Be Light!
P. S. This may be the end of this book, but it certainly is not the end of the story. The light of Gods love and Gods truth continues to shine in dark places, and the Lord our God still speaks from the mountain to all who will listen and believe.

- the author